God W

The Case for
Christian Meditation

Teresa Yerkes

Christian Meditation Center
368 S. Tuckahoe Road
Williamstown, NJ 08094
tyerkes@christianmeditationcenter.org

Ordering Information:

Quantity sales. Special discounts are available on quantity purchases by corporations, associations, and others. For details, contact the publisher at the address above.

Printed in the United States of America

Dedicated to Our Lord and Savior

Our Father,

In the midst of uncertainty, You are with us. There is no place we can go that You are not already there. Deepen our faith, so that we might trust You more.

We come to You with our hearts wide open for whatever You have prepared for us. Minister to us individually according to our needs and Your Will. Draw us closer to You, so that we may be more like You.

Let these words and the meditation of my heart be acceptable in Your sight, O Lord, my rock and my redeemer.

In Jesus' precious name, Amen.

*Immeasurable gratitude to God for
His gift of love and patience.*

*Special thanks to my family and friends
for their love and support.*

The Vision

This book was inspired by the new richness and depth my relationship with God the Father, Christ the Son and Holy Spirit has become since I began the practice of Christian meditation. I became a Christian in the early 80's by accepting Jesus as my Savior and have been on fire for our Lord ever since. There was a whole laundry list of things the Lord needed to clean up in my life. There were unhealthy habits, incorrect thinking and a lot of emotional turmoil regarding my love relationships.

Although I knew I was saved by grace, it was disheartening for my life to be so out of line with His truth. How I wanted to represent Him better; to be a good role model and a light where others could see the goodness of God. How I wanted to experience His freedom and rest promised in the Bible. How I wanted to know His peace that passes all understanding. How I longed to know His love and to be a vessel He could use to love others.

1

Even though I couldn't see these things in my life to the degree I desired them, I had faith He would grant them to me.

So, I remained hopeful for a long time; eighteen years to be exact. I remembered having what I call my *coming to Jesus* moment. A day when I began to lose hope. I wondered if I would ever be free from my old nature. I was so tired of still having the same issues coming up again and again. I was so embarrassed by the lack of self-control I had over certain behaviors.

But by God's mercy, it was on that very day, He invited me to come to Him in a deeper, more intimate way. He wanted me to dwell with Him in the center of my being, and just be still and silent before Him. I did and it was the beginning of a new way of connecting with God.

The following Sunday in church there was an announcement for a class teaching Centering

Prayer. I had already been practicing moving my attention to the center of my being and resting there in His Presence, but I thought maybe there was more for me to learn. So, I attended the class. The class was informative, and I was grateful others were on this same path as well. I began reading books, authored by Christians, on this type of practice. And again, I was grateful to those authors for writing about their experiences. Those men and women gave me hope God would continue to work within me to make me more like Him.

It has been nearly 20 years since I first practiced, what I call, Christian meditation. It has brought me to a place in my walk with God that has allowed me to experience His freedom and rest. I know His peace and His love on a much deeper level. As a matter of fact, the practice of meditation has allowed me to experience the fruit of the Spirit in an expanded way. There was always evidence of love, joy, peace, patience, kindness, goodness, faithfulness, gentleness and self-control in my life, but not like the depth and expansiveness the Spirit of God now expresses through me.

It was shortly after I started practicing, when I sensed I was supposed to do something with the practice of meditation. At first, I thought it was to sell what I call *prayer chairs*; which are kneeling chairs to help support a person's desire to meditate. I worked on that project for a while; without much success. God finally got through to me it was about deepening the relationship with Him that was important, not the chair. Of course, it is funny now, looking back on it, to see the real reason for the passion He placed within me.

Even with knowing His desire, I still didn't know what I should do next. Without knowing the full picture, I started teaching others how to meditate. It was so encouraging to see others having similar experiences I had with the practice. They too were able to know God on a deeper level.

I continued to pray for direction on what He wanted me to do next. There was something within me that knew there was more on the horizon with this passion I had. It took twelve years before I heard the Call to create a non-profit organization called the Christian Meditation Center (CMC). Since February 22, 2012, the CMC has been teaching prayer and meditation, offering retreats, facilitating book clubs, encouraging the reading of scripture, providing Christian counseling and spiritual direction within the local community and beyond.

God has given me a heart to support others on their walk to be more like Him. Meditation is a practice that brings us closer to God, and by the grace of God, be united with Him. Jesus Himself told us the Kingdom of God is within. So, for me, it made sense to seek Him there. For He is as close to us as our very breath. It is in being closer, we find the healing we need and the power to overcome our old nature. I would like to present a case for the need to teach others the practice of Christian meditation within our churches and organizations. The Christian Meditation Center's vision is to see families, friends and neighbors integrating meditation into their daily lifestyle to foster a deeper relationship with God. We see church congregations returning to the practice of meditating, as an integral part of their Christian faith. My hope is, on the following pages, our Lord reveals to your heart the importance of finding time to rest in His presence.

The Rationale

America is having an anxiety crisis. Anxiety has hit an all-time high in our society, within ourselves and within our homes. I am not an expert on anxiety, but here are some statistics experts are telling us. Mental health professionals have classified anxiety into seven main types: Generalized Anxiety Disorder, Social Phobia, Panic Disorder, Agoraphobia, Other Phobias, Post-Traumatic Stress Disorder (PTSD) and Obsessive-Compulsive Disorder (OCD).

The Anxiety and Depression Association of America claims:

- Anxiety disorders are the most common mental illness in the U.S., affecting 40 million adults in the United States age 18 and older, or 18.1% of the population every year.
- Anxiety disorders are highly treatable, yet only 36.9% of those suffering receive treatment.

- People with an anxiety disorder are three to five times more likely to go to the doctor and six times more likely to be hospitalized for psychiatric disorders than those who do not suffer from anxiety disorders.

- Anxiety disorders develop from a complex set of risk factors, including genetics, brain chemistry, personality, and life events.

- Anxiety disorders affect 25.1% of children between 13 and 18 years old. Research shows that untreated children with anxiety disorders are at higher risk to perform poorly in school, miss out on important social experiences, and engage in substance abuse.[1]

On the global front, the organization Our World in Data reported, "The prevalence of anxiety disorders across the world varies from 2.5 to 7

---

[1] Anxiety and Depression Association of America, 2019. Retrieved from https://adaa.org/about-adaa/press-room/facts-statistics.

percent by country. Globally an estimated 284 million people experienced an anxiety disorder in 2017, making it the most prevalent mental health or neurodevelopmental disorder."[2]

It is easy to believe the number of people suffering is much higher because many people either do not seek help, are misdiagnosed, or do not realize they have anxiety and are self-medicating with drugs, alcohol and other addictive behaviors.

People can experience a mild form of anxiety or one that's debilitating. Depending on the severity, we know anxiety can have devastating effects on our families and relationships. It is almost impossible to effectively explain the last-minute

---

[2] Our World in Data, 2018. Retrieved from https://ourworldindata.org/mental-health#anxiety-disorders.

cancellations of attendance at social events, meetings and other pre-arranged appointments. It is hard to find the right words to excuse what appears to be a lack of interest or plain bad manners. And how can we expect people to understand why our brother, wife, mother or son is never seen outside the house. People may wonder, "Do *they really exist*?" And the misinterpretations and false perceptions continually compound the problem.

The resulting family dysfunction caused by anxiety disorders often results in the problem becoming further complicated by the psychological and physical reactions of other family members--the husband who drifts in and out of affairs because his social phobic wife is unable to participate in the social areas of his business life; the teenager who rebels against the restrictive family life imposed by his father's fear of having a panic attack, and ends up involved in drugs and petty crime; the mother who finally suffers a mental breakdown, after years of coping with the manipulations of her anxiety-disordered child. The scenarios are countless.

Anxiety, which stems from fear--robs, steals and destroys our lives and the lives of loved ones. There are over one hundred symptoms and signs for anxiety, panic attacks, and other anxiety disorders. Here are just a few symptoms: Dizziness, chest pain, headaches, neck tension, stomach upset, nervous stomach, pulsing in the ear, fear of impending doom, shortness of breath, heart palpitations, inability to rest, and sleep problems.

Importantly, anxiety disorders are often associated with other serious psychiatric disorders, particularly common, depression, eating disorders, ADHD and substance abuse.[3] So, when one has an anxiety disorder, there's a tremendously increased risk of having one of those other disorders, which will have a serious impact on relationships and functioning.

---

[3] National Institute of Mental Health, 2019. Retrieved from https://www.nimh.nih.gov/health/topics/anxiety-disorders/index.shtml.

The Remedy

Well this can all sound so hopeless, without a remedy...right? But the truth is there is a cure, and His name is Jesus. When you are yoked to Jesus, you are not yoked to restlessness, strife, or worry. Real peace is not the absence of conflict, but the presence of Jesus. I would like to share two passages from the Bible that Jesus has promised us: "Come to me, all you who are weary and burdened, and I will give you rest. Take my yoke upon you and learn from me, for I am gentle and humble in heart, and you will find rest for your souls.[4] And the second passage, "Peace I leave with you; my peace I give you. I do not give to you as the world gives. Do not let your hearts be troubled and do not be afraid."[5] Two truthful statements anchoring us to who we are in Christ, in midst of whatever life throws our way.

---

[4] Matthew 11:28-29 New International Version (NIV)
[5] John 14:27 NIV

Jesus' promise to give us rest and peace has captivated my attention for years. But there was always the nagging question, "Well how do I get them?" I couldn't figure out what was missing. I had an active prayer life. I didn't feel like I was getting very far reading books and commentaries on the subject. They would help for a while, and then I would find myself back into the drama and chaos. There just wasn't a staying power to remain in His peace. It wasn't until I started the practice of Christian meditation that the experience of remaining in his rest and peace, most of the time, was even possible.

Here we find in Matthew 6:25-34, a passage where Jesus is urging his audience not to worry. "Therefore I tell you, do not worry about your life, what you will eat or drink; or about your body, what you will wear. Is not life more than food, and the body more than clothes? Look at the birds of the air; they do not sow or reap or store away in barns, and yet your heavenly Father feeds them. Are you not much more valuable than they? Can any one of you by worrying add a single hour to your life?

And why do you worry about clothes? See how the flowers of the field grow. They do not labor or spin. Yet I tell you that not even Solomon in all his splendor was dressed like one of these. If that is how God clothes the grass of the field, which is here today and tomorrow is thrown into the fire, will he not much more clothe you—you of little faith? So do not worry, saying, 'What shall we eat?' or 'What shall we drink?' or 'What shall we wear?' For the pagans run after all these things, and your heavenly Father knows that you need them. But seek first his kingdom and his righteousness, and all these things will be given to you as well. Therefore do not worry about tomorrow, for tomorrow will worry about itself. Each day has enough trouble of its own."[6]

Jesus clearly tells us not to worry about tomorrow. He is challenging us to stay focused on Today. It is an invitation for us to live in the present moment. Have you ever tried to experience fully what is happening right now? Like right now, you are focused on what you are reading. Let's give this a try...close your eyes and just focus on your breath coming in and going out. Now take one minute to experience the breath coming in and breath going out. Did you notice that you were not worried or anxious during that time? Of course, the exception would be those of you who suffer from performance anxiety. You may have worried about whether you were doing the breathing right. I say that in jest, but the truth is anxiety can rear its ugly head anytime. But most

---

[6] Matthew 6:25-34 NIV

of you were not worried because you were paying attention to what is happening right now.

When you are focused on right now, you are not projecting what might happen in the future. Did you notice you were feeling calmer, maybe even some peace? Now this was just a quick little exercise, but can you imagine how your life would be if you lived in the present moment for longer periods of time, maybe, possibly all the time. This is what Jesus wants for us. As He said, do not worry about the future for each day has enough trouble of its own. And friends, there are people who live this way. Most of them practice resting in the presence of God; which some call Christian meditation.

Let's take this to another level of understanding of how important it is to be in the present moment. Consider this, our natural selves view the function of time as one of extending itself forward. We don't regard ourselves as being in the place of eternity. However, Paul reminds us, "And God raised us up with Christ and seated us with him in the heavenly realms in Christ Jesus."[7] Even so, the natural self will want to stay in a continuum of time, keeping us focused only on the past or the future. But the Holy Spirit is interested in keeping our attention on eternity. It is when we are in the present moment that we are not subject to the past or the future. In other words, our natural selves' desires to keep us in time, where the Holy Spirit's desires our release from it.

Healing begins when we are living in the present moment and not in the past. Our mind cannot produce wellbeing from our past experiences, it can only do so from the present. When healing is experienced in the present, it gives way to a new future.   Can you see that if our minds are in the past, we will keep on experiencing the same old

---

[7] Ephesians 2:6 NIV

things? Being in the present moment breaks the momentum of the past moving us into the future. Therefore, we need to tap into the eternal/present moment to experience a different future.

So, the first strategy is to practice being present, being here now, in this very moment. The practice of Christian meditation naturally reveals the present moment, and over time we begin to live in it more often. The more we are in His Presence, the more His Presence fills us. You will learn more about Christian meditation later in this book.

The second strategy is taking control of our thoughts, so they don't use us to make poor decisions. We all experience unwanted and harmful thoughts and scripture guides us to best manage them. Paul says in 2 Corinthians, "We tear down arguments, and every presumption set up against the knowledge of God; and we take captive

every thought to make it obedient to Christ."[8]
Many of us are yanked around by our thoughts all
day long. We contend with them even when we
are trying to go to sleep. It can feel like we are in
a battle; leaving us rather exhausted. Sadly,
thoughts can have a negative effect on our bodies,
emotions and spirit. The thoughts can be the
driving force to unhealthy lifestyle choices, angry
outbursts, lying, etc. Paul shares in Romans, "I
want to do what is good, but I don't. I don't want
to do what is wrong, but I do it anyway."[9] I believe
we can all relate to his experience.

It takes time to off load our natural selves, so
who we truly are, in Christ, is revealed. One way
to help facilitate that reality, is to take Paul's
advice in Philippians 4:8, "Finally, brothers and
sisters, whatever is true, whatever is noble,

---

[8] 2 Corinthians 10:5 NIV

[9] Romans 7:19 New Life Translation

whatever is right, whatever is pure, whatever is lovely, whatever is admirable--if anything is excellent or praiseworthy--think about such things."

In truth, wayward and worrying thoughts rob us of the peace we are promised. And to make worrying an even less appealing approach to how we process situations, rarely do our projections of the bad things ever really happen. Worrying comes from being afraid and stems from our natural selves, but certainly not from God. As soon as we hear ourselves say "Why is this happening to me?" or "What am I going to do about this situation?", it is time to change our thoughts to, "What is God up to?", "What does He want to teach me?" or "How will He lead me in this situation?" Did you notice how the change in our thinking shifted from worrying--to God is in this with me? We can opt out of the same old worry story we put ourselves into when things don't go according to our plans. A far better story awaits us when we decide to participate in the resting in His peace story. The story where He has our best interest in mind. Aligning with His mind allows us to take control of our thoughts and not be used by them.

Too many people have lost the power to control their thinking. Is it possible we don't believe or trust God to follow through with his promises or bless us when we follow His advice? Or do we want to believe but have been raised in a family of worriers and it has become what we do when situations aren't going the way we have planned. Even if you are not a worrier, it can be difficult to trust the advice Jesus gives us, to be like the flowers and the birds. For we are humans and have a lot of responsibility. We may feel the comparison is not reasonable. Flowers don't have brains and birds don't have to function the same as we do. It doesn't feel like an appropriate comparison. But the point Jesus is making is we too can have the capacity to not worry just like the flowers and birds. His invitation is to trust and rely on Him; to let go of our need to control everything.

Trust is crucial when we begin our journey to practice Christian meditation. It may take time to experience the beauty of resting in His Presence. You may have to rely on other people's experiences with the practice to keep you motivated. It is certainly an exercise of faith; believing He is no respecter of persons.[10] If He is there for others, He will be there for me. Clear evidence for the practice, based on scripture, can be found in the Book of Luke. Jesus said, "Neither shall they say, see here! or, see there! for, behold, the kingdom of God is within you".[11] Some Christians are surprised to know the Trinity is established within themselves. It is equally true

---

[10] Acts 10:34 NIV

[11] Luke 17:21 New King James Version (NKJV)

that God is outside of ourselves and among us. Jesus also tells us to seek first the Kingdom of God and all things will be given to you.[12]

So, let's go on an exploration to find this Kingdom within ourselves. We know it is within us and we know in seeking for it, all things will be given to us. Jesus' teaching also includes instruction on how to seek God's Kingdom, "The time has come, he said. The Kingdom of God has come near. Repent and believe the good news."[13] So, we are called to repent because "all have sinned and fall short of the glory of God".[14] Romans 6:23 adds that "the wages of sin is death, but the gift of God is eternal life in Christ Jesus our Lord."

Our natural way of thinking is contrary to God's way of thinking. Since what we think and believe

---

[12] Matthew 6:33 NIV
[13] Mark 1:15 NIV
[14] Romans 3:23 NIV

can lead to behaviors that are not healthy for us or could lead to compromising our values. Even more of a reason for us to be transferred into the Kingdom to initiate our transformation. Repentance is the realization that my way doesn't work, and you are sorry for all the misguided mistakes and sins that you have committed. An important next step is to accept the forgiveness God has given you through His Son Jesus and trust that the Holy Spirit will lead and guide you to wholeness. This is the necessary first step to open us up to our spiritual selves. For by one sacrifice He has made perfect forever those who are being made holy.[15]

Once we accept that Christ died on the cross to eradicate our sins, we are forgiven, our sins are forgotten, and our spirit is quickened or made alive within us. We read in the Book of Colossians, "You

---

[15] Hebrews 10:14

were dead in sins, and your sinful desires were not yet cut away. Then he gave you a share in the very life of Christ, for he forgave all your sins, and blotted out the charges proved against you, the list of his commandments which you had not obeyed. He took this list of sins and destroyed it by nailing it to Christ's cross. In this way God took away Satan's power to accuse you of sin, and God openly displayed to the whole world Christ's triumph at the cross where your sins were all taken away."[16] Your citizenship transferred from the Kingdom of this world, which is darkness and fear-based, to the Kingdom of God, which is light, and love-based. As Colossians 1:13-15 tells us, "For He has rescued us from the dominion of darkness and brought us into the Kingdom of the Son He loves, in Whom we have redemption, the forgiveness of sins."[17] We are now sons and daughters of God and our new

---

[16] Colossians 2:13-15 Living Bible (TLB)

[17] Colossians 1:13-15 NIV

home is the Kingdom of God. It is our fresh start to live our life through Christ. This is the Good News!

Jesus was "anointed to proclaim freedom for the prisoners and recovery of sight for the blind, to set the oppressed free, to proclaim the year of the Lord's favor."[18] For those of us who have accepted this good news, our testimonies tell of a time when we were once lost, but now we are found. Once blind, but now we see. However, that is only partially true experientially. The truth is more like *once we were blind*, but now we squint. For we don't see who we truly are right away. "For now we see in a mirror, dimly, but then we will see face to face. Now I know only in part; then I will know fully, even as I have been fully known."[19] We don't see who we are in Christ fully--it is revealed to us

---

[18] Luke 4:18-19 NIV
[19] 1 Corinthians 13:12 NKJV

over time. That is why the next step is so important.

During this time, we will recognize the movement and teaching of the Holy Spirit. Jesus said, "And I will ask the Father, and he will give you another advocate to help you and be with you forever—the Spirit of truth.[20] The Spirit gives us a spirit "of power and of love and a sound mind."[21] This is when our personal resurrection begins. As we rise, all that limits our divine potential are removed. "For in Christ there is all of God in a human body; *so you have everything when you have Christ,* and you are filled with God through your union with Christ. He is the highest Ruler, with authority over every other power."[22]

---

[20] John 14:16-17 NIV

[21] 2 Timothy 1:7 NKJV

[22] Colossians 2:9-10 TLB

So it is apparent from our current human experience something more needs to happen. That something more we find in this wonderful verse, "He (John is referring to Christ) must increase, but I must decrease."[23] And this is what the increase should look like according to scripture, "But the fruit of the Spirit is love, joy, peace, patience, kindness, goodness, faithfulness, gentleness and self-control. Against such things there is no law."[24] And the decrease is all that limits the fullness of God from being experienced in our lives. And this is how the conversion, from what limits us--to the fullness of Christ, as we are known by God, takes place.

Jesus tells us, "Remain in me, as I also remain in you. No branch can bear fruit by itself; it must remain in the vine. Neither can you bear fruit unless you remain in me. I am the vine; you are the

_____

[23] John 3:30 NKJV
[24] Galatians 5:22-23 New English Translation NET

branches. If you remain in me and I in you, you will bear much fruit; apart from me you can do nothing."[25]   The truth is when we move our attention away from God, we lose our awareness of His Presence and His Peace.

Remaining in Him and knowing who we are in Him places us in alignment to bear much fruit. It is important to know who we are in Christ. We need to know and believe what our true nature is. How hard it would be for us to bear fruit if we didn't believe or feel worthy to come into alignment with God. But if we don't, we will continue with the same old behaviors because we have the same old incorrect belief systems. You will find a list of some of the scriptures describing our true nature in Appendix A.

Not only does our natural self limit the fullness of God from being our experience, it also prevents

---

[25] John 15:4-5 NIV

us from perceiving the world correctly. If there is error in our beliefs, we will have errors in our thinking--which create errors in our behavior. However, if we remain in the Kingdom, and rely on the Holy Spirit to guide us, we will see with greater clarity. When we choose the Spirit as our guide, we begin to live in the will of God, and we will bear much fruit.

A question asked often is, "What is the Will of God?" When reflecting on our Lord's prayer, what did Jesus mean by "Your Kingdom come, Your will be done on earth as it is in heaven."[26] Christ wouldn't have asked us to pray this prayer unless it was possible to experience the Kingdom now. How can it be on earth as it is in heaven? The only way I can think this could be so, is if God's will is directed through Christ who is within us.   We certainly cannot obtain God's Kingdom on earth as

---

[26] Matthew 6:10 NIV

it is in heaven, until it is established first within ourselves; likeness creates likeness.

Our openness to allow Him to work through us will determine either a Kingdom or a worldly existence. This is what Christ modeled for us when He said in the Garden of Gethsemane, "Not my will, but your Will be done." We find all through the life of Christ, He had a close relationship with God the Father. He would often go off to some solitary place to be with God alone. His mind was always about doing what God told Him to do. And so, it will be with us. Our wholeness becomes established within us when we recognize and embrace the truth that our will is His Will. But until we, by the grace of God, do that—we will find that running the show our way will limit our ability to live in His Peace. We can't have it both ways. You would think it would be the most coveted exchange program available to mankind, my will for His will. Sadly enough, our will wins out more times than not. And when it does, we become distracted and move away from His peace.

What are some of the ways we become distracted from His peace? The Word of God provides some insight. You keep him in perfect peace, whose mind is stayed on you because they trust in you.[27] So, we could say the opposite is true as well. We will lose our perfect peace, experientially speaking, when our mind is not on God. There are two ways peace can withdraw from our awareness. The first is when our natural selves or our false interior landscape takes over. What is so troubling about our natural selves is that we are not always aware when we are participating in fear-based or self-preservation behavior. And secondly, when the world, our false exterior landscape, takes over. We sometimes think it is our circumstances that move us away

---

[27] Isaiah 26:3 NKJV

from peace, but actually it is how we manage and react to our circumstances that move us away from peace. The quality and consistency of our peace is measured by the degree of Christ's fullness available within us. Paul tells us in I Corinthians, we have the mind of Christ.[28] Therefore, it is important for us to be present in the mind of Christ.

Here are some beliefs and attitudes that keep our minds off Him:

1. Believing we know better than God.
2. We resist what the current reality is.
3. We judge others and situations.
4. We have found our pseudo peace through alcohol, drugs, sex, food, gambling, etc.
5. Believing lies instead of truth.
6. Believing God won't live and work through us.
7. Believing God didn't get something right.

---

[28] 1 Corinthians 2:16 NKJV

8. Believing the things of this world will lead us to happiness.
9. Believing God isn't interested in making us whole or doesn't want us to experience His Peace.
10. Allowing fear to drive behavior. Fear-based thinking might sound like this:
    a. I am not adequate.
    b. I have no self-control.
    c. I am worthless.
    d. I don't want to or can't change.
    e. I don't have enough.
    f. I can't let others see my flaws.
    g. I may lose opportunities.
11. Believing we are not who God says we are. When we identify with our natural selves and not our true selves.

These are some of the behaviors when we believe in error. We...

a. blame our mistakes on others.
b. want others to think we are special because of our job, what we own, education, our looks, athletic ability, etc.
c. are more concerned with how another perceives us than with the person.

d. need to be recognized for things we do and become angry or upset if we don't get it.

e. boast about our accomplishments.

f. look for attention by talking about our problems.

g. expect others to think and be like us.

h. share our opinions when no one has asked.

i. flatter others for self-gain.

j. use anger to shut down another's thoughts or feelings.

k. take things personally.

l. feel offended when others think differently.

m. complain about how others are wrong and the reasons we are right.

n. want to be seen or to appear important.

Our mind filters what we see through what we believe. We need to believe differently--to see differently. Marcel Proust says it this way, "The real voyage of discovery consists not in new landscapes, but in having new eyes."[29] In other words, we don't need our circumstances to change

---

[29] Marcel Proust (1871-1922), was a French novelist, critic, and essayist.

as much as we need to see our circumstances from the mind of Christ.

Our natural selves will fight to keep these false belief systems in place. Our response, as stated before should be, "We demolish arguments and every pretension that sets itself up against the knowledge of God, and we take captive every thought to make it obedient to Christ."[30] Being aware of the beliefs we have about God can keep our natural selves in check. When we take a closer look at these beliefs, we find they are contrary to love. Love is our guide. The easiest way to know we are being loving is to check our motives. We should strive for selfless motives, not selfish ones. When we are self-giving with our love, we have a mature love.

Being intentional about walking in love daily will eliminate fear-based beliefs. There is no fear in

---

[30] 2 Corinthians 10:5 NIV

love. But perfect love drives out fear, because fear has to do with punishment. The one who fears is not made perfect in love.[31] In that one verse alone, John has given us the secret for driving out fear. We need to increase our capacity to love. The best way to do that is to ask God to fill us with His Love. As we receive it, give it away so that more will come to you. I encourage you to pray for His love daily. There is no power greater than the power harnessed in love.

So other than cultivating a truthful belief system, beliefs anchored in love, one other practice will help us expand the fruit of the Spirit within us, is meditation. I am not discounting or downplaying the importance of prayer, I am only emphasizing meditation because most of us know how to pray. Connecting with God in any way is a very good practice.

---

[31] 1 John 4:18 NIV

Meditation supports our need to be centered and to just rest in the presence of God without an agenda. Both prayer and meditation are essential in enhancing our relationship with God. Good communication, however, needs to go both ways. You can look at meditation as the other side of prayer. When we pray, we are talking to God. When we meditate, we become open to listen to God. We know it's difficult to have a loving and meaningful relationship with anyone if we did all the talking all the time. Meditation establishes the two-way interaction for a deeper, more receptive and richer relationship with our Lord.

Meditation is a powerful practice that expands the Fruit of the Spirit within us. Expands, bringing a more refined, enhanced quality to the experience of the Fruit that doesn't leave us as our situations change. These attributes become a stable state of being and not fleeting emotions. This is how you will experience the resurrection or the fullness of Christ opening within you. You will experience more and more of the fullness of Christ. Paul reminds us, "I have been crucified with Christ and I no longer live, but Christ lives in me."[32]

This is a journey and as we continue to cooperate with the leading of the Holy Spirit, we will find that meditation changes how we live our lives. We gradually begin to see using the eyes of Christ. We may experience healing of our physical bodies, our emotions and mental faculties. As a side note, we may experience these things if we don't meditate, but with meditation you will notice a much more refined quality of who you are. You could call it a higher level of consciousness. I felt as if meditation accelerated the resurrection of Christ within me. I experienced the refined qualities of Fruit of Spirit as a stable condition. This new state started to develop within several

---

[32] Galatians 2:20 NIV

months of practicing meditation. A deeper relationship developed between the Lord and me. I found myself becoming healthier within my heart, soul and mind. I felt free and able to make decisions that aligned with my values.

Another reason meditation is so powerful is because when we place our attention on God, we are unable to pay attention to all the thoughts that stream across our mind. It allows us to explore the center of our inner being where our true peace resides within the Kingdom. God's presence is always with us. However, we are not always aware of it. Discovering your Center is like explorers finding new territory; the territory was always there, but we didn't know it existed. Finding it can best be expressed in the parable Jesus taught about the hidden treasure and the pearl. "The kingdom of heaven is like treasure hidden in a field. When a man found it, he hid it again, and then in his joy went and sold all he had and bought

41

that field. Again, the kingdom of heaven is like a merchant looking for fine pearls. When he found one of great value, he went away and sold everything he had and bought it."[33]   My understanding of *sold everything he had,* to mean letting go of our old nature and the path we are on to find happiness, so we are available to embrace the new treasure.

The evidence of how valuable this practice is can be found among those who are practicing meditation regularly. They would encourage you to spend time within the Kingdom, to just rest and be with our Lord. The practice of meditation transports us to the Center of our inner being; the Kingdom of God. Meditation is only the vehicle to bring you there. The Holy Spirit will help navigate your way there. Once you find your way, you will find it easier to return. Each time we return, we

---

[33] Matthew 13:44-46 NIV

enter our Eternal Home. After we have entered often, we will notice we carry the heavenly residue of our visit back into our daily lives. This heavenly residue fuels the expansion for our capacity to walk by the Spirit, so we don't gratify the desires of the flesh.[34] This is how we are to be in the world, but not of it.

There are several ways to practice meditation. I practice and teach only one way. You will find my practice in Appendix B. It doesn't matter how you discover the Kingdom of God within. Just find a way to meditate that works for you. You may find it easy to incorporate the practice into your prayer time, scripture reading, daily devotions or journaling. It is easiest to meditate following any time you are already experiencing God from your heart. Whether you are praying, journaling, reading scripture or your daily devotions. Since

---

[34] Galatians 5:16 NIV

you are already with Him, just stop the talking or activity and remain in His Presence in silence. Consider lingering there for a while and be still and know He is God.[35] If you find you are distracted by your thoughts or outside noise, gently return to the Kingdom.

Here are some suggestions on how to approach meditation:

1. We believe He desires a deeper and richer relationship with us.
2. We come with no agenda or desiring anything but Him.
3. Our intention is to rest in the stillness, silence and spaciousness of our inner being—the Kingdom of God.
4. Our attitude should be one of attentiveness and love; a silent worship.
5. Invite Him to do whatever is needed to make us more like Christ.

---

[35] Psalm 46:10 NIV

6. "Being confident of this, that He who began a good work in you will carry it on to completion."[36]

7. "Therefore, since we are receiving a kingdom that cannot be shaken, let us give thanks, by which we offer to God an acceptable worship with reverence and awe; for indeed our God is a consuming fire."[37]

Indeed, let us be grateful! My hope is you believe you are ready to take this journey to the Center to find out for yourself what awaits within the Kingdom. I can assure you that you won't be disappointed. I can tell you for most people it is not an easy discipline to stay with. We are not oriented to be still for long periods of time. If you are task oriented, you may lose your desire to practice because at times it feels like you aren't doing anything. We may also be discouraged when we find our minds have kidnapped us from

---

[36] Philippians 1:6 NIV
[37] Hebrews 12:28-29 NRSV

our desire to spend time with God. Take heart, even if you find yourself thinking about things and you must return your attention back to God a hundred times—what other time during the day do you return to God so many times? That's why it's called a 'practice' my friend! We keep returning, so that one day we will just be there. Maybe this is what Paul had in mind when he gave instruction to "pray without ceasing."[38]

If you haven't received Christ as your Savior and you feel the Spirit of God is touching your heart to do so, let me share a prayer you can say to invite God, Christ and the Holy Spirit to come and live within you.

Father, I know that I have broken your laws and my sins have separated me from you. I am truly sorry, and now I want to turn away from my past sinful

---

[38] 1 Thessalonians 5:17 NRSV

life toward you. Please forgive me and help me avoid sinning again. I believe that your Son, Jesus Christ died for my sins, was resurrected from the dead, is alive, and hears my prayer. I invite Jesus to become the Lord of my life, to rule and reign in my heart from this day forward. Please send your Holy Spirit to help me obey You, and to do Your will for the rest of my life. In Jesus' name I pray, Amen.

Welcome to the Kingdom of God! Now go spend time with the Father, Son and Holy Spirit. They have been waiting for you.

ABOUT THE

CHRISTIAN MEDITATION CENTER

My story, leading to the founding of the Christian Meditation Center, began many years ago. I had been a Christian for seventeen years; yet found myself dealing with obstacles that came between myself and a closer relationship with God. I was really struggling with painful emotional issues and a lifelong addiction to alcohol. I felt frustrated and defeated. Frankly, I felt unworthy to be called a child of God. Even though there had been many victories, such as quitting smoking, healing in other relationships and spiritual breakthroughs, I was still unable to feel right with God. I wanted to feel whole and totally in control of my thoughts and actions. I knew this was possible because the scriptures told me so. I wanted my reality to mirror the Fruits of the Spirit, which are love, joy, peace patience, kindness, goodness, faithfulness, gentleness and self-control.

And then the answer came! One day sitting in my family room God made it clear to me that he wanted me to spend time with Him in stillness and silence. I knew that he was calling me to a more intimate relationship with Him. This began my journey to experience the presence of God. I was drawn to many Christian authors that wrote about contemplation, meditation, quiet prayer, centering prayer and other genres associated with this practice of just being still and quiet before the Lord. I also began a regular practice of resting in the Lord by moving my attention out of my head and just focused on my breathing. During this time, I learned to stay open to allow God to move in me any way He saw fit. I started to see amazing positive changes in my personality and demeanor. People began to comment on the peace and the calmness they saw in my life. I no longer had obsessive thoughts that defeated me emotionally. God removed in me the desire to drink alcohol and through His peace I was finally able to overcome the addiction.

Throughout this time, God has placed on my heart this yearning to share this path to a closer relationship with Him to others. I knew that if it was successful in my own Christian walk that it might help others understand and ultimately heal the issues in their lives that prevent them from sharing the same peace that the still and quiet time alone with God has brought me. I realized that God was about to use me for His will and was directing me on a journey to find a way to share meditation with others. It was over twelve years of praying and seeking advice from others before God showed me the way.

Then it happened, God placed it in my heart, we needed to start a nonprofit organization to serve as the vehicle to teach his people how to meditate and develop a closer relationship with Him. Subsequently, the nonprofit business, Christian Meditation Center was formed. Now the journey expands, with Christ minded brothers and sisters helping to share the power of meditation to anyone who wants to have a more intimate relationship with God.

THE FOUNDER AND AUTHOR

TERESA YERKES

 **Teresa Yerkes**, the Founder of Christian Meditation Center, has been a Christian since 1983 and has practiced Christian meditation since 2000. She is the author of the book, "Making Love: The Spiritual Act of Love. She teaches and leads seminars and retreats. Teresa is a Certified Lay Speaker and Lay Counselor. She brings nearly forty years of her own personal discovery, along with highly specialized spiritual direction training provided by the Shalem Institute.

CHRISTIANMEDITATIONCENTER.ORG

tyerkes@ChrisitanMeditationCenter.org

You can find us on Facebook, Twitter and Tumblr.

NOTES

1. Anxiety and Depression Association of America, 2019. Retrieved from https://adaa.org/about-adaa/press-room/facts-statistics.
2. Our World in Data, 2018. Retrieved from https://ourworldindata.org/mental-health#anxiety-disorders.
3. National Institute of Mental Health, 2019. Retrieved from https://www.nimh.nih.gov/health/topics/anxiety-disorders/index.shtml.
4. Marcel Proust (1871-1922), was a French novelist, critic, and essayist: Light a Fire, 2019. Retrieved from https://www.lightafire.com/marcel-proust-biography/478/.
5. Bible Gateway, 2019. Retrieved from https://www.biblegateway.com/.

Appendix A

MY TRUE NATURE IN CHRIST

This is a short list of the many attributes we possess in Christ; Who is our True nature.

I am complete in Him who is the head of all principality and power. -Colossians 2:10

I am the light of the world. -Matthew 5:14

I am a partaker of His divine nature. – 2 Peter 1:3-4

I am free from the law of sin and death. -Romans 8:2

I am delivered from the power of darkness and translated into God's kingdom. -Colossians 1:13

I can do all things through Christ who strengthens me. -Philippians 4:13

I am more than a conqueror through Him who loves me. -Romans 8:37

I am raised up with Christ and seated in heavenly places. – Ephesians 2:6; Colossians 2:12

I am greatly loved by God. -Romans 1:7

I have the mind of Christ. -1 Corinthians 2:16

I am alive with Christ. – Ephesians 2:5

I am an ambassador for Christ. -2 Corinthians 5:20

I am a new creation in Christ. -2 Corinthians 5:17

I am God's workmanship, created in Christ for good works. -Ephesians 2:10

I have the Greater One living in me; greater is He who is in me than he who is in the world. -1 John 4:4

I am forgiven of all my sins. -Ephesians 1;7

I am His elect, full of mercy, kindness, humility, and longsuffering. -Romans 8:33; Colossians 3:12

I have the peace of God that passes all understanding. -Philippians 4:7

Appendix B

Christian Meditation – The practice to discover your center and to rest in the presence of God. (meditate for 20 - 30 minutes)

1. Sit up straight, shoulders back, chest area open, resting your hands comfortably in your lap.
2. Pray the Lord's Prayer.
3. Your attitude should be one of gratitude towards life. Lift a prayer of gratitude and thankfulness for all God has provided for you. Invite God to open your heart and soul to do His will. Surrender your will to His love and care, so He can make you more like Him.
4. If you are already praying from your heart and not your mind, just stop talking and remain in His Presence in silence and stillness.
5. If you are praying from your mind, begin to focus on your breathing, the breath moving in out of your lungs, for several minutes. Stay alert and relaxed. We should have an open, attentiveness during the meditation. This will help you move into the present moment. Then move your focus on your heart for several minutes. Feel like a child, feel your heart light and full of love. Let go of any distractions;

including thoughts, emotions or images and just unwind.

6. If your attention draws you back to your mind and you find you are thinking about your thoughts, just **gently** return to your breath.

7. To go deeper interiorly, silently say *deeper*. Since you will move deeper interiorly, you don't need to move back to the surface to return to your breath. At this stage, just notice your breath; the breath of God breathing in you. Remain in the silence and stillness within you.

8. At the end of your meditation time, end your meditation by saying *Amen*. With your eyes still closed, take a couple of minutes to bring yourself back to your surroundings. Thank God for all He has done for you during this time together.

9. As you go through your day, bring the love and peace you experienced with you.

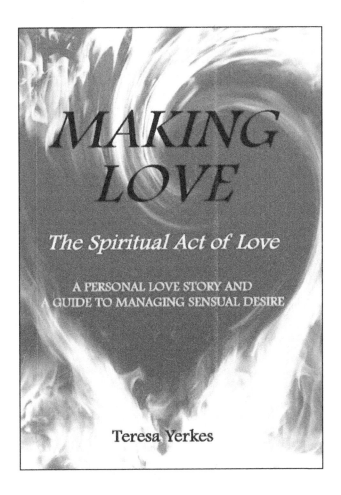

Made in the USA
Monee, IL
14 October 2022

15859166R00036